The Life, Myths, and Wisdom of Lord Shiva

The Eternal Dance

vimladeepak

DEDICATION

To my dearest friends and family,

Your unwavering support and belief in me have been the guiding lights on this literary journey. Through every twist of the plot and every turn of the page, your encouragement has fuelled my passion for storytelling. This book is as much yours as it is mine.

To the readers,

Thank you for embarking on this adventure with me. May these pages offer you escape, inspiration, and perhaps a touch of magic. Your imagination breathes life into these words, and for that, I am endlessly grateful.

With love and gratitude,

Vimladeepak

Preface

In the vast tapestry of Hindu mythology, few deities evoke as much reverence, wonder, and philosophical depth as Lord Shiva. He is the destroyer, the creator, and the preserver, all intertwined in one divine persona. Known for his asceticism, compassion, and cosmic dance—the *Tandava*—Shiva embodies the cycles of life, death, and rebirth. Yet, beyond the mythological framework, Shiva is the formless consciousness that transcends time and space, symbolizing the infinite and the unknowable.

This book, *The Life, Myths, and Wisdom of Lord Shiva: The Eternal Dance*, seeks to unravel the enigma of Shiva through the many stories, legends, and teachings that have been passed down through the ages. From his origins in ancient Vedic texts to his vibrant presence in temples and festivals today, we explore the multifaceted nature of this deity, understanding how each tale carries profound wisdom.

Shiva's eternal dance is not merely a myth; it is a metaphor for the dance of life itself—the harmonious interplay of creation and destruction, joy and sorrow, attachment and renunciation. It invites us to see beyond the superficial layers of existence and perceive the deeper truths that govern the universe.

As we embark on this journey into the heart of Shiva's mythology and teachings, let us not only seek knowledge but also cultivate the wisdom he represents: the wisdom of letting go, of finding balance within chaos, and of embracing the divine within ourselves.

May this exploration inspire you to experience the eternal dance that unfolds within all of us.

Content

Introduction 1

The Origins of Shiva 5

Shiva's Role in the Trinity (Trimurti).................... 11

Shiva's attributes and symbols.......................... 16

The Marriage of Shiva and Parvati 21

Shiva's Meditation and Anger 26

Shiva and the Demon Tripurasura 34

Mahashivaratri...41

Shiva's Role as the Ascetic (Yogi) 47

The story of Mohini and Shiva.........................53

Shiva's Dance of Death 60

Shiva and Karma 63

The Divine Feminine Energy 69

The Symbolism of the Lingam.........................76

Popular Temples 80

Daily Worship Practices of Lord Shiva.................104

Shiva in the Modern World............................110

Conclusion 112

Introduction

Welcome to the World of Lord Shiva

This book, *The Life, Myths, and Wisdom of Lord Shiva. The Eternal Dance*, invites you on an enthralling journey into the life, symbolism, and profound wisdom of one of the most revered deities in Hinduism—Lord Shiva. Known as "The Destroyer" in the holy trinity of Brahma, Vishnu, and Shiva, he represents both the destruction of ignorance and the creation of new life, embodying the eternal cycle of birth, death, and rebirth. His myths, legends, and philosophies have captivated devotees and scholars for millennia, as they offer insights into the deepest mysteries of the universe, consciousness, and the self.

This book aims to explore not only Shiva's divine attributes but also the life lessons hidden in his stories. For those unfamiliar with Hindu mythology, Shiva's symbolism might seem complex, but it holds universal truths that transcend culture and religion. Whether it's his meditative stillness, the cosmic dance of creation and destruction, or his deep association with time and transformation,

Shiva's stories offer timeless guidance on navigating life's challenges and embracing personal growth.

A Glimpse into Hindu Mythology:

Hinduism, one of the world's oldest religions, is often described as polytheistic, meaning it features many gods and goddesses. However, it is also deeply rooted in the idea of one ultimate reality, called Brahman, which manifests through various deities. These deities represent different aspects of life, nature, and the cosmos, allowing devotees to connect with the divine in many forms.

Lord Shiva holds a central place in this vast pantheon. While gods like Brahma create and Vishnu preserve, Shiva is the force that brings change. His role is not simply to destroy but to clear the path for renewal and transformation. From his wild, ascetic lifestyle in the Himalayas to his cosmic dance, the "Tandava," Shiva's myths reflect both the fierce and compassionate aspects of existence. His consort, Parvati, and his children, Ganesha and Kartikeya, weave into these stories, making Shiva not just a destroyer but a symbol of family and balance between the personal and the cosmic.

Understanding Lord Shiva means delving into the very core of Hinduism, where mythology, philosophy, and spiritual practice intertwine, offering insights into the universe and one's inner self. Whether you are new to Hindu thought or already familiar, the myths and wisdom surrounding Shiva offer profound lessons for navigating the complex dance of life.

Chapter 1

The Origins of Shiva

Shiva, one of the principal deities of Hinduism, has a multifaceted presence in ancient Indian texts, including the Vedas and the Puranas, which document his earliest forms and evolving significance. Though he is most prominently featured in later Hindu scriptures, his origins can be traced back to the Rigveda (one of the oldest Vedic texts, composed between 1500-1200 BCE). In these texts, he appears in the form of Rudra, a fierce and stormy god.

Rudra is described as a deity who brings destruction through storms and disease but also offers healing and protection. Over time, Rudra's image gradually merged with that of Shiva, who became known as the Mahadeva (Great God) and a more benevolent and all-encompassing figure. The Shvetashvatara Upanishad, dating back to around 400-300 BCE, also plays a pivotal role in the transition of Rudra into Shiva. This Upanishad extols Rudra as the Supreme Being, referring to him as the creator, preserver, and destroyer of the cosmos—a role that later becomes a central aspect of Shiva's identity.

The Puranas, particularly the Shiva Purana and Linga Purana, further solidify Shiva's stature as both creator and destroyer. In these texts, he is often depicted in his Nataraja form, performing the cosmic dance (Tandava), which symbolizes the cycle of creation, preservation, and dissolution of the universe.

Shiva's power of destruction is seen not as malevolent but as a necessary force to maintain the balance of existence, preparing the universe for regeneration.

Creator and Destroyer

Shiva's dual role as creator and destroyer emphasizes his transcendence over time and space, functioning as a cosmic force that initiates and ends cycles of existence.

He embodies the paradox of life, holding within himself both the serenity of creation and the chaos of destruction.

This duality is a key feature of Shaivism, where Shiva is regarded as the ultimate reality that manifests itself in the balance of opposites—life and death, light and darkness, creation and dissolution.

The Cosmic Dancer

In the heart of the universe, where time and space dissolve, Shiva performs his eternal dance—the Tandava, a rhythmic and powerful movement that sets the universe into motion. As his feet strike the ground, worlds are created, and as his arms swirl through the cosmic air, they destroy them, returning them to the primordial void. This is not a dance of chaos, but one of harmony, representing the cycle of birth, life, death, and rebirth.

Shiva's cosmic dance represents the rhythm of existence, and through its motions, he maintains the balance between creation, preservation, and destruction. His dance is witnessed by the gods, humans, and all living beings as the divine play that dictates the natural order.

At the center of this dance, Shiva's third eye blazes, symbolizing his transcendent wisdom, which pierces through illusion. In one hand, he holds a damaru (drum), whose beats resonate as the pulse of life. In another hand, he carries fire, the flame of destruction that consumes ignorance and old forms, clearing the way for regeneration. As Shiva dances, the cosmic order is maintained, and the universe is in perfect balance. He dances for eons, embodying the eternal truth that creation and destruction are intertwined, two parts of the same divine force. His dance reminds all beings that change is the law of the universe and that in destruction lies the seed of new life.

This portrayal of Shiva as the cosmic dancer highlights his supreme control over the destiny of the cosmos, acting not only as its destroyer but also as its rejuvenator. This dance symbolizes the interplay of energy and matter, the birth and death of worlds, and the endless cycle of existence that continues through the eons, all under Shiva's watchful and timeless gaze.

Chapter 2

Shiva's Role in the Trinity (Trimurti)

In Hinduism, the Trimurti represents the three main aspects of the divine cosmic functions: creation, preservation, and destruction. The Trimurti consists of Brahma, Vishnu, and Shiva, who are responsible for maintaining the cycle of the universe.

- **Brahma** is the creator who brings forth life and the cosmos.
- **Vishnu** is the preserver, maintaining balance and order in the universe.
- **Shiva** is the destroyer and transformer, overseeing the cycle of death and rebirth.

Shiva as the Destroyer and Transformer

Shiva's role as the destroyer is often misunderstood as something negative. However, in Hindu philosophy, destruction is not the end; it is a necessary step for regeneration and renewal. Destruction clears the way for new creation and transformation. As the transformer, Shiva facilitates this continuous cycle of birth, life, and death, ensuring the universe evolves.

Shiva's role also symbolizes the destruction of illusions (Maya) and ignorance, enabling spiritual enlightenment. His cosmic dance, the Tandava, represents the dynamic forces of creation, preservation, and destruction at play in the universe.

The Churning of the Ocean (Samudra Manthan)
One of the most famous stories that highlights Shiva's transformative and protective powers is the Samudra Manthan, or the Churning of the Ocean. The gods (Devas) and demons (Asuras) sought the nectar of immortality (Amrita) hidden in the depths of the ocean. To obtain it, they decided to churn the ocean together, using Mount Mandara as the churning rod and the serpent Vasuki as the rope. As they churned, many precious and powerful substances emerged, but so did a deadly poison called Halahala.

The poison was so potent that it threatened to destroy all of creation—both the gods and demons were powerless to stop its spread. In desperation, they turned to Shiva, the great destroyer, and asked him for help.

13 | The Eternal Dance

Shiva, out of compassion for all living beings, agreed to drink the poison. However, instead of swallowing it, he held it in his throat to prevent its harm. His wife, Parvati, stopped the poison from descending into his body by pressing his throat. As a result, Shiva's throat turned blue, earning him the name Neelkanth, meaning the "Blue-Throated One."

This act of self-sacrifice demonstrated Shiva's immense power and compassion, as he saved the universe from destruction by neutralizing the deadly Halahala. The churning continued, and eventually, the nectar of immortality was retrieved.

Symbolism

- **Shiva as Protector**: Shiva's willingness to drink the poison highlights his role as the protector of creation, stepping in during times of cosmic danger.
- **Transformation**: The story emphasizes transformation, both physical (Shiva's blue throat) and cosmic, as it showcases how destruction and danger can lead to a higher purpose, protecting the world and allowing new beginnings.

Shiva's role in the Trimurti is thus central to the balance of the universe, where destruction is an essential part of creation, leading to renewal and transformation.

Chapter 3

Shiva's attributes and symbols are rich in meaning, reflecting profound philosophical and spiritual ideas. Each element of his form represents a deeper aspect of life and the cosmos, tying into awareness, power, and the balance of destruction and healing.

1. Shiva's Third Eye

- **Symbolism**: The third eye of Shiva is a powerful symbol of inner vision, wisdom, and higher consciousness. It is believed to be the source of his ultimate perception beyond ordinary senses, representing his ability to see beyond the physical world, perceiving truth and reality in their entirety.

- **Philosophical Idea**: This eye represents *awareness* or *enlightenment*, showing Shiva's capacity to understand the underlying nature of the universe and human existence. When opened, it is said to release fire, which destroys illusion and ignorance, purifying the world through destruction.

2. The Serpent Around His Neck

- **Symbolism**: Shiva is often depicted with a coiled serpent (usually a cobra) around his neck. Serpents are symbols of both fear and power, and in Hinduism, they represent rebirth, transformation, and the cyclical nature of life due to their ability to shed their skin.

- **Philosophical Idea**: The snake around Shiva's neck represents *mastery over fear and death*. Shiva, being beyond time, remains unaffected by the deadly and fearsome aspects of life, including death itself. The serpent symbolizes Shiva's control over primal energy, especially kundalini (the primal life force), and his power to transcend time and death.

3. The Ganga Flowing from His Hair

- **Symbolism**: The river Ganga flowing from Shiva's matted hair represents the divine river Ganges, which is considered the holiest river in Hinduism. According to legend, when the river descended from the heavens, its force was so great that Shiva caught it in his hair to prevent its destructive power from annihilating the earth.
- **Philosophical Idea**: The Ganga represents *life, purity, and sustenance*. Flowing from

Shiva's hair, it shows the aspect of Shiva as the sustainer and protector of life. It also represents the idea of *controlled power*, as Shiva can contain and channel this immense force for the benefit of all.

4. Shiva's Blue Throat (Neelkanth)

- **Symbolism**: The blue throat is a direct reference to the legend of the churning of the ocean (Samudra Manthan), during which a deadly poison, Halahala, emerged. To save the universe from destruction, Shiva drank the poison, holding it in his throat to prevent it from spreading, which turned his throat blue.

- **Philosophical Idea**: The blue throat symbolizes *sacrifice and selflessness*. Shiva's act of swallowing the poison represents the idea that destruction, when controlled, can save and heal. It highlights the dual nature of Shiva—both the destroyer and protector—and his willingness to bear suffering for the greater good.

5. Philosophical Insights

- These symbols together represent the dual nature of Shiva as both a destroyer and a healer. The third eye signifies his power to destroy ignorance and illusion, the serpent reflects his mastery over primal fears, and the Ganga and his blue throat showcase his ability to channel destructive forces into life-giving and protective energy. This duality is central to Shiva's role in the cosmic cycle of creation, preservation, and destruction.

- Shiva's attributes remind devotees of the deeper truths of existence: *awareness*, the *transience of life*, the *power of transformation*, and the importance of *sacrifice for the greater good*.

These symbols, while associated with destruction, ultimately point to the path of healing and transcendence, demonstrating Shiva's role as a force of cosmic balance.

Chapter 4

The Marriage of Shiva and Parvati: A Tale of Contrasting Energies

The union of Shiva, the god of destruction, and Parvati, the goddess of fertility and love, is a cornerstone of Hindu mythology. This paradoxical pairing symbolizes the intricate balance between opposing forces in the universe.

The Divine Matchmaker:

It is said that Parvati, in her previous incarnation as Sati, had sacrificed herself to save her father, Daksha, from the wrath of Shiva.

The Tragic Tale of Sati

Before her incarnation as Parvati, Sati was the daughter of Daksha, a powerful sage and progenitor of the Devas (gods).Sati was deeply devoted to Shiva and often accompanied him to his ascetic retreats in the Himalayas.

Daksha, however, was jealous of Shiva's growing popularity and held a grudge against him. He organized a grand sacrifice (yagna) but deliberately excluded Shiva and his followers.

Sati, feeling insulted, decided to attend the yagna despite her father's objections.

When Sati arrived at the yagna, she was treated with disrespect and humiliated by Daksha and his guests. Unable to bear the insult, Sati immolated herself in the sacrificial fire. Shiva, upon hearing of his beloved wife's death, became consumed with rage. He unleashed his destructive powers, destroying Daksha's yagna and killing many of the Devas.

Shiva's destructive rampage caused great chaos in the universe. To restore order, the gods intervened and convinced Shiva to calm down. However, the trauma of Sati's death had a profound impact on Shiva, leading him to withdraw into deep meditation and isolation.

It was in response to Shiva's grief and the need to restore balance in the universe that Sati was reincarnated as Parvati, a goddess of unparalleled devotion and beauty. Parvati's determination to win Shiva's heart and restore their union is a central theme in Hindu mythology.

Moved by her devotion, Shiva vowed to never marry again. However, Parvati, determined to win his heart, reincarnated as Parvati and performed rigorous austerities to attract his attention.

The Divine Test

Impressed by her devotion, Shiva decided to test Parvati's resolve. He disguised himself as a fearsome demon named Tarakasura, who terrorized the world. When Parvati heard of the demon's atrocities, she prayed to Shiva for help. To her surprise, Shiva appeared before her in his true form, revealing his divine nature.

The Divine Wedding

Moved by Parvati's unwavering faith and love, Shiva agreed to marry her. A grand wedding ceremony was held, attended by all the gods and goddesses. The union of these two seemingly contradictory deities symbolized the harmony between the forces of creation and destruction, the spiritual and the material.

The Significance of the Union

The marriage of Shiva and Parvati holds profound significance in Hindu mythology. It represents:

- **The balance of opposites:** The union of the destroyer and the creator symbolizes the eternal cycle of life and death, creation and destruction.

- **The power of devotion:** Parvati's unwavering devotion to Shiva ultimately won his heart, demonstrating the transformative power of love and faith.

- **The divine feminine:** Parvati's role as the divine feminine energy complements Shiva's masculine energy, creating a harmonious balance in the universe.

The story of Shiva and Parvati's marriage serves as a powerful reminder that even the most contrasting energies can coexist and create something beautiful. It is a testament to the intricate tapestry of life, where opposing forces work together to maintain the cosmic order.

Chapter 5

Shiva's Meditation and Anger

The story of the birth of Lord Ganesha is rich with symbolism and provides deep insights into Lord Shiva's nature, emotions, and cosmic responsibilities. Here's a more detailed exploration:

1. Parvati's Creation of Ganesha

The story begins with Parvati, who, while longing for companionship during one of Shiva's long meditative absences, creates Ganesha. She fashions him from the dirt of her own body and breathes life into him. This act is significant as it represents the maternal power of creation and nurture. Ganesha becomes a part of her, both literally and symbolically, acting as her loyal son and protector.

The creation of Ganesha without Shiva's involvement also highlights Parvati's independence and her role as a goddess capable of birthing life. This act reflects her autonomy in the cosmic dance of creation, which is an essential part of her identity.

2. Shiva's Return and the Conflict

When Shiva returns from his deep meditation, his mindset is completely detached from worldly affairs. Shiva's meditative state is symbolic of his transcendence and aloofness from mundane attachments and emotions. His anger upon being blocked by Ganesha reflects his role as a divine being who doesn't tolerate obstacles on his path. Shiva's fury in this moment can be seen as a cosmic reflex, the natural reaction of a force of destruction and renewal. Ganesha, unknowing of his father's power and position, stood as a literal obstacle in Shiva's path, resulting in Shiva's destructive wrath. The act of beheading is symbolic of Shiva's power over life and death – a reminder that destruction is an essential part of the cosmic cycle of creation, preservation, and dissolution.

3. The Beheading and Parvati's Grief

The moment of Ganesha's beheading is central to understanding Shiva's complex emotions. In a split second of anger, he beheads his own son, and this impulsive act represents the volatility of Shiva's destructive aspect. The beheading could be interpreted symbolically as the destruction of ignorance or the ego, a theme common in many Shiva stories. In his rage, Shiva doesn't recognize Ganesha as his son, further emphasizing that in moments of pure destruction, the personal or the emotional is often suspended in favor of divine will. Parvati's grief and fury upon discovering what had happened is another pivotal moment in the narrative. She represents the powerful force of creation, and her sorrow threatens to destroy the universe, showcasing how deeply intertwined the forces of creation and destruction are. This part of the story symbolizes the feminine power (Shakti) in balance with Shiva's masculine force, demonstrating the unity and balance required in the universe.

4. Shiva's Remorse and the Elephant Head

Shiva's remorse at Parvati's grief marks a turning point in the story. While his anger led to destruction, his compassion and love lead to creation – a key duality in Shiva's character. He immediately seeks to undo the damage caused by his fury, ordering his attendants to bring him the head of the first creature they find, which happens to be an elephant.

The attachment of the elephant head symbolizes renewal and transformation. Ganesha's new form – part human, part animal – illustrates the idea of overcoming ego (symbolized by the head) and embracing divine wisdom. Elephants, known for their strength, wisdom, and memory, are an apt symbol for Ganesha, who would later become the remover of obstacles and the god of intellect and wisdom.

5. Shiva as a Father

One of the most compelling aspects of the story is Shiva's evolution as a father. Initially detached, focused solely on his cosmic role, Shiva fails to recognize his connection to Ganesha. But through Parvati's grief and his own regret, Shiva's paternal instincts emerge, transforming him from a wrathful destroyer to a compassionate and repentant father. This transformation highlights Shiva's depth of emotion, which transcends the typical godly detachment. His ability to show regret and take corrective action displays his understanding of love and responsibility, even in his position as a cosmic force. In many ways, this story humanizes Shiva, making him relatable as a father who makes mistakes but is willing to amend them.

6. Deeper Symbolism

- **The Elephant Head**: The elephant symbolizes wisdom, strength, and auspiciousness. Ganesha's new head makes him the god of intellect and learning, while also symbolizing humility – a large head and ears representing the need to listen more and speak less.

- **Shiva's Anger**: Shiva's anger in this context isn't just a destructive force; it also represents righteous indignation. The beheading of Ganesha can be interpreted as the removal of ignorance (the head being a metaphor for ego). The subsequent replacement of Ganesha's head with an elephant's represents the idea of divine intellect replacing the ego.
- **Balancing Creation and Destruction**: Shiva's act of destruction (beheading) is followed by an act of creation (reviving Ganesha), showing his dual role as the destroyer and the creator. This story emphasizes that destruction is not always the end, but a necessary step for renewal and transformation.

7. Lessons from the Story

- **Control Over Anger**: Shiva's wrath is a reminder of the consequences of uncontrolled anger. While Shiva, as a divine being, can correct his mistakes, humans are not always afforded the same luxury, making this a cautionary tale about acting impulsively.

- **Forgiveness and Redemption**: Shiva's regret and efforts to restore Ganesha's life demonstrate the importance of forgiveness and redemption. Even divine beings can make mistakes, but what matters is how they rectify them.

- **Balancing Duty and Love**: Shiva's actions reflect the delicate balance between divine duty and personal love. Though he is a god with cosmic responsibilities, he is also a father, bound by emotions and love. The story reminds us that duty and emotions are not mutually exclusive but must be navigated carefully.

Conclusion

The story of the birth of Ganesha and Shiva's subsequent wrath and redemption paints a complex portrait of Lord Shiva as both a cosmic force and a loving father. His actions reflect the tension between destruction and creation, divine duty and personal responsibility, anger and compassion. Through the restoration of Ganesha's life, Shiva not only reconciles his relationship with his son but also teaches valuable lessons about the nature of life, emotion, and cosmic balance.

Chapter 6

Shiva, in Hindu mythology, is not just the god of destruction but also a protector of the cosmos.

His role as the slayer of evil highlights how he maintains balance in the universe by eliminating forces that cause harm and chaos. One of the most thrilling examples of this is the story of Shiva and the Demon Tripurasura, which clearly shows how Shiva destroys evil not for the sake of destruction, but to allow new beginnings and restore balance.

Shiva and the Demon Tripurasura

Once upon a time, in the ancient realms where gods and demons often clashed, there lived three powerful asuras—Tarakaksha, Vidyunmali, and Kamalaksha. These three brothers were not like ordinary demons. They were immensely skilled, intelligent, and ambitious, with hearts set on gaining ultimate power.

From a young age, they performed severe penances, praying to Lord Brahma, the creator of the universe, who was known for granting boons to those who showed great devotion. Pleased by their devotion, Brahma appeared before the three brothers.

"Ask what you wish," Brahma said, his voice echoing with divine authority.

The brothers, eager to rule the cosmos, had already thought about their wish.

"Grant us three cities," they said, "one made of gold, another of silver, and the last of iron. Let these cities roam freely in the heavens, unbound by the earth. And let us be immortal—except for one condition. Let us only be destroyed when all three cities align in a straight line, and even then, only by a single arrow."

Brahma, though wise, saw no immediate harm in their request. He granted the boon and disappeared. Soon after, the brothers set about building their magnificent cities—Tripura, the Three Cities.

The first city, made of shimmering gold, floated high above the heavens, dazzling all who saw it. It was the residence of Kamalaksha, the eldest brother, who ruled with unmatched splendor. Below him was the second city of silver, where Vidyunmali resided, his city gleaming like the moon across the sky. The last city, forged of iron, was ruled by Tarakaksha, and it roamed the earthly realms, casting a long shadow over the lands below.

For years, the Tripurasura ruled over their cities, traveling the cosmos at will, untouched by any foe. Their power grew with each passing day, and so did their arrogance. As time went on, the brothers began to believe that their might was unmatched, even by the gods themselves. Soon, they unleashed terror upon the worlds. They attacked the heavens, enslaved mortals, and disrupted the natural order of the universe.

The gods, led by Indra, the king of the heavens, grew desperate. No matter how many armies they sent, they could not defeat the Tripurasura. The three cities, with their unique protections, could not be destroyed unless they aligned, and that would only happen once in a thousand years. Even then, the cities could only be destroyed with a single, perfect shot.

In their despair, the gods turned to Lord Shiva, the Supreme Destroyer, for help.

"Shiva," they pleaded, "the Tripurasura have become too powerful. They threaten the balance of the universe. Only you can stop them."

Shiva listened to the gods' request, his eyes half-closed in deep thought. The Tripurasura were indeed fierce and powerful, but they were also devotees of Brahma, and Shiva, who valued devotion, hesitated.

"I cannot destroy them without cause," Shiva said, his voice calm but firm. "They have done no wrong to me directly."

But as time passed, the asuras' tyranny grew unbearable, even to Shiva. Finally, when the destruction they caused threatened to unravel the very fabric of creation, Shiva agreed to put an end to them.

The time came when the three cities, by the design of fate, aligned perfectly. It was the moment the gods had been waiting for. Shiva prepared for battle. To aid him, Vishvakarma, the celestial architect, crafted a magnificent chariotfor him. It was no ordinary chariot—it had the Earth as its base, the Sun and the Moon as its wheels, and the Vedas (sacred texts) as the horses that pulled it forward.

Shiva, in his fearsome form of Tripurantaka, took his place in the chariot. In his hands, he held a divine bow, forged by the gods themselves. The arrow he prepared was no ordinary weapon—it was imbued with the collective energy of all the gods, including Lord Vishnu, whose power radiated from the tip.

As the cities aligned in the sky, the moment of destruction arrived. The gods held their breath as Shiva drew the bowstring back, his eyes fixed on the three cities. With a single motion, swift as thought, Shiva released the arrow. It shot through the heavens with the force of a thousand storms, streaking toward the aligned cities.

In an instant, the arrow pierced through all three cities—gold, silver, and iron—at once. There was a great explosion of light and sound, as the cities crumbled and fell into the cosmic waters below. The reign of the Tripurasura was over.

With the destruction of the Three Cities, the universe was restored to balance. The gods rejoiced and praised Shiva for his supreme act of destruction. However, Shiva did not revel in his victory. He had only done what was necessary to preserve the cosmic order.

The story of Tripurasura became one of the most famous legends in the lore of Lord Shiva, a reminder of the inevitable fall of those who misuse power and disturb the balance of the universe. It also stood as a testament to Shiva's unmatched might, who, though calm and detached, would destroy even the most powerful when the world required it.

Thus, the tale of the Tripurasura and the Three Cities faded into legend, but its lessons of arrogance, power, and divine justice endured through the ages.

Shiva's destruction of Tripurasura teaches us that ending one chapter of life is often necessary for a new beginning. Just like Shiva's arrow that clears away evil to bring peace, our personal challenges and struggles often pave the way for fresh opportunities and growth.

In essence, Shiva's destruction of the demon cities is a reminder that every ending is a doorway to something new. Destruction, whether in the universe or in our lives, is not final—it is a transformative process that leads to renewal and balance.

Chapter 7

Mahashivaratri, often referred to as "The Great Night of Shiva," is one of the most significant festivals dedicated to Lord Shiva.

Celebrated annually in the Hindu month of Phalguna (February or March), it is a night of profound spiritual importance for devotees of Shiva. The festival holds immense significance due to its deep connection to the cosmic aspects of Lord Shiva's personality, including his role as the destroyer, transformer, and restorer of the universe.

Spiritual Significance of Mahashivaratri

1. **The Cosmic Dance of Creation and Destruction**

   Mahashivaratri is believed to be the night when Lord Shiva performs the divine dance, the Tandava, symbolizing the cycle of creation, preservation, and destruction. This cosmic dance represents the dynamic and regenerative forces of the universe, with Shiva embodying the dissolution of old energies to make way for renewal.

2. **Union of Shiva and Parvati**

   Many devotees also celebrate Mahashivaratri as the day when Lord Shiva married Goddess Parvati, symbolizing the merging of masculine and feminine energies.

This union represents balance and harmony in the universe, as well as in personal relationships.

3. **A Night of Spiritual Awakening**

   The night is considered highly auspicious for meditation and spiritual awakening. It is said that the energies on this night are aligned in such a way that one's spiritual growth is accelerated. Devotees believe that staying awake all night helps them harness this cosmic energy and enhances their spiritual practice.

4. **Overcoming Darkness and Ignorance**

   Mahashivaratri is symbolic of overcoming ignorance and darkness in life. Shiva is often associated with the annihilation of ego and ignorance, which prevents spiritual growth. The night-long vigil and fasting are acts of surrender to the divine, allowing individuals to rise above material distractions and connect with higher consciousness.

Why Devotees Stay Awake All Night?

Staying awake on Mahashivaratri is not just a ritual but a form of dedication to the worship of Lord Shiva.

1. **Spiritual Vigilance**:
   The all-night vigil, called Jagaran, represents a state of heightened awareness and the transcendence of sleep, which symbolizes ignorance. Devotees remain alert to receive Lord Shiva's blessings and attain spiritual enlightenment.

2. **Cosmic Alignment and Energy Flow**:
   According to yogic tradition, the night of Mahashivaratri holds a special energy that is conducive to spiritual growth. Staying awake and meditating during this night helps devotees absorb the beneficial cosmic energy.

3. **Imitating Lord Shiva's State**:
   Shiva is often referred to as the "eternal yogi," one who is always in a state of meditation and transcendence. By staying awake, devotees aim to imitate Lord Shiva's ability to remain detached from worldly desires and fully engaged in spiritual consciousness.

4. **Celebrating Shiva's Role in the Universe**:
   The night vigil is a way to honor Lord Shiva's role as the destroyer of evil and ignorance.

It is believed that staying awake during this night helps devotees overcome inner darkness and find divine light.

On Mahashivaratri, devotees fast, meditate, chant Shiva mantras like Om Namah Shivaya, and visit temples to offer prayers. The lingam, which symbolizes Lord Shiva, is bathed with milk, honey, and water as part of the ritual worship, symbolizing purification and the washing away of sins.

This festival is a profound celebration of Lord Shiva's role in the cosmic cycle and an opportunity for devotees to deepen their connection with the divine, purify their souls, and experience the transformative power of Shiva's grace.

Chapter 8

Shiva's Role as the Ascetic (Yogi)

Shiva is revered in Hinduism as the supreme ascetic, embodying the virtues of renunciation, self-discipline, and spiritual wisdom. His identity as a yogi, often depicted sitting in deep meditation atop Mount Kailash, emphasizes his detachment from material pleasures and worldly attachments.

Shiva's lifestyle as an ascetic transcends the physical plane; he is shown wrapped in a tiger skin, smeared with ash, and with matted hair. Each of these elements reflects the purity and austerity of a yogic life, free from material desires, emphasizing spiritual liberation.

Mount Kailash, Shiva's spiritual abode, is not just a physical place but a symbol of the highest state of consciousness. It is where he meditates, immersed in the vastness of the cosmos, disconnected from the distractions of the world. The mountain represents the unshakable stillness and vastness of the soul, a place that stands between the earthly and the divine realms. Shiva's existence as a yogi atop Kailash signifies the highest level of spiritual achievement—moksha, or liberation from the cycle of birth and death.

His deep meditations demonstrate an extreme form of yogic discipline—an ability to withdraw all of his senses and mind from the external world, focusing solely on the divine. He embodies *vairagya*, or detachment, the core principle of asceticism, where even the pleasures and pains of life cannot disturb the inner peace and balance of the soul. This state of renunciation allows Shiva to transcend the cycles of time and space, residing in a state of pure consciousness.

The Tale of Shiva's Deep Meditation

There is a famous tale of how Shiva once entered a deep meditative trance that lasted for eons. After a long battle, Shiva retreated to Mount Kailash to meditate. He became so deeply engrossed in his inner consciousness that he completely withdrew from the world. Seasons passed, civilizations rose and fell, but Shiva remained unmoved, lost in the divine dance of the universe within him.

As Shiva meditated, the cosmos began to feel his absence. The balance between creation, preservation, and destruction was disrupted. Without Shiva's conscious presence, the forces of the universe began to spiral out of control. The gods became anxious as his prolonged meditation disturbed the natural order. Destruction loomed, as the universe was starved of Shiva's dynamic energy, his *Shakti* (divine power).

Concerned for the world's welfare, Parvati, Shiva's wife and the embodiment of cosmic energy, sought to awaken him. Despite his immersion in his trance, she knew that only her loving touch could bring him back. Ascending Mount Kailash, she approached him gently, placing her hand on his heart. Slowly, Shiva opened his eyes. Though he had returned to the material world, his face still carried the calm and serenity of one who had touched infinity. Shiva smiled, realizing the universe's need for his presence, but his essence remained grounded in the wisdom of his meditation.

This tale reflects the delicate balance Shiva maintains between his roles as the destroyer and as the yogi. Even while withdrawing into the stillness of meditation, his divine purpose remains linked to the maintenance of universal harmony.

The Value of Stillness and Introspection in a Chaotic World

The story of Shiva's deep meditation and his role as the supreme yogi offers profound insights into the power of stillness and introspection in our lives. In today's fast-paced and chaotic world, where constant activity, noise, and distractions dominate, Shiva's example teaches us the importance of stepping back from the rush of life and seeking stillness within ourselves. His ability to retreat into deep meditation represents the idea that true wisdom and peace come from within, not from external circumstances.

Shiva's meditation reflects the essence of *pratyahara* in yoga—the withdrawal of the senses from the external world to focus on the inner self. This concept is especially relevant in our modern lives, where constant engagement with technology, work, and societal demands can overwhelm our senses and minds. By practicing detachment, much like Shiva, individuals can cultivate inner calm and mental clarity, allowing for greater introspection and self-awareness.

Stillness, as symbolized by Shiva's meditative state, also teaches us to be patient. Shiva's long meditation while the world waited mirrors how sometimes, we too need to pause, reflect, and gather our strength before we can re-enter the world with renewed clarity and purpose. In his deep introspection, Shiva finds alignment with the divine consciousness, demonstrating how periods of silence and reflection are not times of inactivity but of profound internal transformation.

In essence, the theme of stillness and introspection in the story of Shiva's deep meditation speaks to the need for balance in our lives. Just as Shiva is both the meditative ascetic and the force behind creation and destruction, we too can find harmony between our active, external roles and our need for quiet reflection.

Chapter 9

The story of Mohini and Shiva

The story of Mohini and Shiva is a fascinating tale from Hindu mythology that showcases Shiva's interaction with Vishnu's avatar Mohini. This story appears in various texts, including the Puranas, most notably in the Bhagavata Purana, the Shiva Purana, and the Skanda Purana. It illustrates the themes of divine play (leela), illusion (maya), and the complex relationship between Shiva and Vishnu, two of the most powerful deities in Hinduism.The Story of Mohini and Shiva

The story begins after the churning of the ocean (Samudra Manthan), a cosmic event in which the gods (Devas) and demons (Asuras) collaborated to churn the ocean to obtain Amrita, the nectar of immortality. When the Amrita finally emerged, a fierce struggle broke out between the gods and demons over who would consume it. To protect the nectar and ensure that it only reached the gods, Vishnu assumed the form of Mohini, a stunningly beautiful woman.

Mohini's beauty was so enchanting that the demons were completely mesmerized by her, and without hesitation, they handed over the Amrita to her, believing that she would distribute it fairly. However, Mohini cleverly gave all the nectar to the gods, leaving the demons empty-handed.

Shiva, having heard of this extraordinary incident and Mohini's unparalleled beauty, became curious. Despite being a great ascetic, detached from the material world, Shiva wanted to witness Vishnu's captivating form as Mohini. Accompanied by his wife Parvati, Shiva approached Vishnu and requested to see the Mohini form.

Vishnu, smiling, agreed and transformed into Mohini in front of Shiva and Parvati. As soon as Shiva saw Mohini, he was immediately enchanted by her beauty. Despite his renunciation and asceticism, Shiva was overcome by desire and started to follow her, captivated by her divine illusion. Mohini, in her enchanting form, playfully led Shiva through the forest, while Parvati watched in astonishment.

Eventually, after a while, Vishnu ended the illusion, and Shiva regained his composure. He laughed at himself, realizing that even he, the greatest ascetic

and master of self-control, could be swayed by
Vishnu's power of illusion (*maya*). This incident
further deepened the respect and bond between
Shiva and Vishnu, showing the balance between
asceticism and the seductive power of illusion.

This story carries profound symbolic and philosophical meanings:

1. **The Power of Maya (Illusion)**: The tale highlights the power of illusion, or *maya*, which even the greatest of ascetics like Shiva cannot completely escape. Mohini represents the divine illusion that captivates and deludes even those who are detached from worldly desires. It serves as a reminder that in the material world, even the most spiritually advanced beings are susceptible to illusion.

2. **Shiva's Humility**: Shiva's reaction after the experience with Mohini is one of humility. He recognizes the power of Vishnu's illusion and does not hold any resentment or pride in being momentarily overcome by it. Instead, Shiva's laughter at the end symbolizes his acknowledgment of the playfulness of the divine and his acceptance of the cosmic forces beyond even his control.

3. **The Divine Play (Leela)**: The entire episode can be seen as part of the divine play or *leela*, where the gods interact with each

other in ways that reveal deeper truths about the universe. Shiva and Vishnu's relationship is one of mutual respect, and this incident reflects their complementary roles in the cosmos. Shiva is the great renouncer and destroyer, while Vishnu is the preserver, often using illusion and beauty to maintain cosmic order.

4. **The Balance of Masculine and Feminine Energies**: Mohini represents the divine feminine energy, or *Shakti*, in its most enchanting form. The interaction between Shiva and Mohini underscores the balance between masculine and feminine energies in the universe. Shiva, who is often associated with austerity, power, and control, is momentarily influenced by the feminine energy of attraction and allure.

In some versions of the story, it is also mentioned that the union between Shiva and Mohini resulted in the birth of a divine being, Ayyappa (or Shasta), a widely revered deity in South India, especially in Kerala, where he is worshiped at Sabarimala. Ayyappa is considered the son of both Shiva and

Vishnu (in Mohini's form), symbolizing the unity of these two great deities.

The story of Mohini and Shiva is a powerful illustration of the play of illusion and divine energies in Hindu mythology. It shows that even deities are subject to cosmic forces, but they also transcend these experiences to reveal deeper spiritual truths. The story reinforces themes of humility, the complexity of desire, and the ongoing cosmic dance between creation, preservation, and destruction.

Chapter 10

In Hindu cosmology, Lord Shiva is revered as *Mahakaal*, the Lord of Time. Time, in its relentless march, governs all existence—ushering birth, growth, decay, and death. However, Shiva transcends this cycle. As *Mahakaal*, he is beyond the confines of time, witnessing its effects but never bound by them. His mastery over death and impermanence symbolizes the ultimate truth: that everything in the universe is temporary, except for the eternal soul and the divine.

Shiva's Dance of Death

The Tandava, one of the most powerful depictions of Shiva's role as *Mahakaal* is his cosmic dance, the *Tandava*. This dynamic and forceful dance embodies the rhythms of the universe itself. Through this dance, Shiva not only creates the cosmos but also sustains and eventually dissolves it. The *Tandava* is often seen as the Dance of Death, where Shiva's movements signify the destruction necessary for new creation.

In Hindu mythology, when Shiva performs the *Tandava*, the universe trembles.

This is not merely a dance of destruction, but one of transformation. It represents the cyclical nature of existence: creation (Srishti), preservation (Sthiti), and dissolution (Samhara). Everything that comes into existence must, in time, fade away—only to be reborn in a new form.

Shiva, as *Mahakaal*, reminds us of the impermanence of life. His role as the Destroyer is not to be feared, but to be understood as an essential force in maintaining balance. Life and death are two sides of the same coin, and without one, the other cannot exist. The acceptance of death is a profound theme in Shiva's mythology. By embracing death, one comes to appreciate the transient nature of life and the beauty of change. Just as Shiva's dance marks the end of one cycle and the beginning of another, we too must accept that death is not an end, but a transition—a gateway to something new. It teaches that nothing is permanent, not even our fears or sorrows. Understanding this inevitability can free one from the anxieties of time and open the path to spiritual awakening.

Chapter 11

Shiva, as the supreme deity in Hinduism, is deeply connected to the concept of *karma*–the universal law of cause and effect that governs all actions. Lord Shiva embodies the idea that through devotion, right action, and deep meditation, one can transcend bad karma and attain liberation (*moksha*). While Shiva is often seen as the Destroyer in the cosmic trinity (Trimurti), his role as the destroyer extends to the dissolution of accumulated negative karma, allowing for spiritual growth and renewal.

Shiva and Karma

Shiva's connection to karma is unique because he does not judge good or bad in a human sense. Instead, he responds to the sincerity of devotion and purity of intent. He rewards those who practice righteous action (*dharma*), devotion (*bhakti*), and deep meditation (*dhyana*). Through these, one can cleanse their soul of bad karma. His grace, often referred to as *anugraha*, is transformative–it has the power to nullify the karmic consequences of past misdeeds.

Shiva's cosmic dance, the *Tandava*, is symbolic of the cyclical nature of creation, preservation, and destruction, much like the cycles of karma that bind individuals to the material world. However, through Shiva's grace, one can break free from these cycles, achieving liberation.

Shiva's Boons and Curses

Shiva's role in shaping the destiny of humans and demons through his boons and curses is a powerful reflection of his connection to karma. Let's look at two famous stories to illustrate this:

1. The Story of Ravana

Ravana, the ten-headed demon king of Lanka, was a great devotee of Lord Shiva. Through intense penance and devotion, Ravana pleased Shiva, who granted him boons of immense power and near invincibility. Ravana's devotion, though sincere, was also tainted by ego and greed. With his newfound strength, he began to misuse his power, creating havoc across the universe. Despite his devotion, Ravana's negative karma began to accumulate as he violated dharma.

Shiva's blessing, when misused, became part of Ravana's eventual downfall. His karma led to his death at the hands of Lord Rama.

This story illustrates that while Shiva rewards
sincere devotion, he also respects the law of
karma—if one strays from the path of
righteousness, their negative karma will bring

consequences, no matter how powerful they have become through Shiva's blessings.

2. The Story of Bhasmasura

Bhasmasura, a demon, performed intense austerities to please Shiva. When Shiva appeared, Bhasmasura asked for a dangerous boon: the power to turn anyone into ashes simply by placing his hand on their head. Shiva, bound by the sincerity of Bhasmasura's penance, granted the boon.

However, Bhasmasura, intoxicated by power, tried to use the boon on Shiva himself. Shiva, realizing the demon's intent, fled, eventually enlisting Vishnu's help. Vishnu, in the guise of a beautiful woman (Mohini), tricked Bhasmasura into placing his hand on his own head, reducing himself to ashes.

In this story, Shiva's boon was both a reward and a curse. It shows how one's actions (*karma*) after receiving a blessing determine the outcome of their destiny. Bhasmasura's greed and arrogance led to his destruction, despite being empowered by Shiva.

Shiva's boons and curses are tied to an individual's karma and intentions. If a boon is misused or accompanied by negative actions, the individual's karma brings its own repercussions.

On the other hand, those who sincerely practice devotion and meditate upon Shiva can erase their bad karma and be freed from its cycle.
Shiva's unpredictable nature serves as a reminder of the delicate balance between power, responsibility, and the consequences of one's

actions. His blessings, when received with humility, lead to salvation; when paired with arrogance, they invite destruction.

In essence, Shiva embodies the cosmic law of karma—rewarding those on the path of dharma and offering liberation to those who seek it through devotion, meditation, and righteous action.

Chapter 12

The concept of Shiva and Shakti embodies the profound idea of cosmic balance, symbolizing the inseparable union of masculine and feminine energies. In Hindu philosophy, Shiva represents the divine masculine, embodying consciousness, stillness, and the unmanifest potential of the universe. Shakti, on the other hand, symbolizes the divine feminine energy—vibrant, dynamic, and creative. Together, they illustrate the complementary forces that sustain the cosmos.

The Divine Feminine Energy

Shakti is the personification of energy, power, and creation. Without Shakti, Shiva would be inert, passive, and transcendent without form or movement. This is why Shakti is often described as the animating force of Shiva, bringing life and manifestation to his formless essence.

Parvati, Durga, and Kali are different manifestations of Shakti, representing different aspects of feminine power:

- **Parvati**: Symbolizes love, fertility, and devotion. She represents the nurturing and compassionate aspects of feminine energy.
- **Durga**: The fierce protector, embodying courage and strength, she combats evil forces and restores balance.

- **Kali**: The powerful and transformative aspect of Shakti, Kali represents the destructive force that annihilates ego and ignorance, making way for renewal.

Ardhanarishvara:

The Tale of Shiva and Parvati as One

The concept of Ardhanarishvara—a composite form of Shiva and Parvati, where they are depicted as one being, half male and half female—beautifully illustrates the unity of opposites.

The right half of the body is Shiva, the masculine energy, and the left half is Parvati, the feminine force. This form transcends physical gender and reveals the deep spiritual truth that all dualities in the universe are essentially unified.

Masculine and feminine, creation and destruction, stillness and movement—each complements the other, making the whole greater than the sum of its parts.

Story of Ardhanarishvara

According to one popular legend, Parvati once questioned Shiva about the nature of their union and why they appeared separate.

Shiva explained that they were never truly apart, but rather, two halves of the same whole. To demonstrate this truth, Shiva merged their forms into Ardhanarishvara, where their combined energies flowed in perfect harmony. This divine form symbolizes that creation cannot happen without the union of both forces.

The story of Ardhanarishvara represents the balance and harmony of dualities in the universe—masculine and feminine, creation and destruction, activity and rest. It also signifies the understanding that both aspects must coexist in equilibrium to sustain life and the cosmos. This unity is not just a metaphor for gender equality but a deeper spiritual truth about the nature of existence.

It teaches that life is a dance between opposites, and only in their unity can we find completeness. In this context, Shiva is often depicted as Shava (a corpse) without Shakti, illustrating that consciousness alone, without energy, is inert. Similarly, Shakti without Shiva is chaotic and uncontained. Together, they create a symphony of existence, where everything in the cosmos moves in a rhythm of dualities—light and dark, joy and sorrow, birth and death.

This divine union is not only a philosophical idea but also a spiritual goal, encouraging individuals to balance the masculine and feminine principles within themselves.

It teaches that the path to enlightenment requires the harmonizing of action and contemplation, love and strength, intellect and intuition.

In essence, Ardhanarishvara represents the oneness of all beings, where every fragment of the universe is a reflection of the greater whole.

Chapter 13

The worship of the Shiva Lingam holds deep symbolic and spiritual significance, representing the formless, infinite aspect of Lord Shiva. The Lingam, often seen as a pillar or oval-shaped structure, is a manifestation of the divine energy that transcends human perception and form.

It encapsulates both the cosmic and the earthly realms, serving as a bridge between these two dimensions.

The Symbolism of the Lingam

- **Formlessness and Infinity**: The Lingam signifies the unmanifest aspect of Shiva, representing the infinite nature of existence and the cosmos. Unlike anthropomorphic deities, the Lingam's lack of distinct features symbolizes that the divine is beyond form, gender, or description. This formless aspect connects to the idea that Shiva is both the creator and destroyer of the universe, cycling life through creation, preservation, and dissolution.

- **Cosmic Connection**: The Lingam is believed to embody the cosmic pillar, the axis mundi, that holds the universe together. It represents the essence of life, the primordial energy that pervades the cosmos, and the source of all creation. In this way, it transcends time and space, uniting the celestial with the earthly. The upright structure of the Lingam symbolizes the ascending energy that connects the physical world (earth) to higher planes of existence (heaven).

- **Union of Shiva and Shakti**: Often, the Lingam is depicted with a Yoni, representing the feminine energy or Shakti. This symbolizes the cosmic balance and unity of opposites–Shiva (consciousness) and Shakti (creative energy). Their union is what generates the universe and sustains it. Thus, the Lingam stands for not just Shiva, but the entire cycle of creation and dissolution, fueled by divine masculine and feminine energies working together.

Sacred Worship of the Lingam

Worshipping the Shiva Lingam involves rituals that invoke the presence of Shiva as the eternal cosmic energy. Through the use of water, flowers, and light, devotees seek to connect their earthly existence to the divine, recognizing their role in the vastness of the cosmos.

1. **Abhishekam**: The act of pouring water, milk, or honey over the Lingam represents the continuous flow of cosmic energy. This ritual is not only an offering but also an acknowledgment of the infinite energy that flows through all beings and the universe itself.

2. **Meditation on the Formless**: The Lingam encourages worshipers to meditate beyond physical forms and personal identities. It is an invitation to experience the divine in its purest essence, without the limitations of mind and body.

The worship of the Shiva Lingam highlights the connection between the cosmic and earthly realms. On a personal level, it serves as a reminder that the divine energy flows through all beings, linking the microcosm (individual soul) to the macrocosm (the universe). On a cosmic level, the Lingam represents the source of creation, the formless beginning from which all things emerge and to which they return.

Thus, the Shiva Lingam stands as an eternal symbol of unity, encompassing both the vastness of the cosmos and the intimate energy within each individual. Through its worship, devotees honor the sacred cycle of life, death, and rebirth, transcending the limitations of form and connecting to the infinite.

Chapter 14

Popular Shiva Temples

1. Kashi Vishwanath Temple (Varanasi, Uttar Pradesh)

The Kashi Vishwanath Temple is one of the most revered and sacred temples dedicated to Lord Shiva. Located in the ancient city of Varanasi (also known as Kashi), it is a symbol of eternal spiritual energy and divine connection. The temple holds an iconic position in Hinduism as one of the twelve Jyotirlingas, which are considered the holiest Shiva shrines. Pilgrims from all over the world visit this temple to seek Lord Shiva's blessings and attain Moksha (spiritual liberation). The significance of Kashi lies in the belief that the city itself is a manifestation of Lord Shiva's presence, making it a prime destination for spiritual seekers.

Mythological Significance

According to Hindu mythology, Varanasi is considered one of the oldest living cities in the world, with its origins going back thousands of years. It is believed that Lord Shiva himself resided here, and that those who die in Varanasi attain salvation and freedom from the cycle of birth and death. The name "Vishwanath" means "Ruler of the Universe," and the temple enshrines the deity as the cosmic overseer.

Kashi is also believed to be the "City of Light" (Kashi means light), where Lord Shiva imparts divine knowledge. The temple has been mentioned in various ancient texts and scriptures, making it a cornerstone of Hindu spirituality.

Architectural Features

The temple complex is a striking example of North Indian temple architecture. The main shrine houses the black stone Jyotirlinga of Vishwanath, which is adorned with flowers and garlands. The golden spire (referred to as the Golden Shikhara) of the temple is one of its most famous features, built using tons of gold donated by Maharaja Ranjit Singh in the 19th century.

The Kashi Vishwanath Temple is surrounded by smaller shrines dedicated to other deities, including Vishnu, Parvati, and Ganesh. The temple is built in a quadrilateral pattern, with narrow lanes (called galis) leading to the main entrance. The proximity to the holy river Ganges adds to the divine atmosphere of the place.

The Kashi Vishwanath Temple is a hub for spiritual rituals and religious ceremonies:

- **Abhishekam**: The most important ritual here is the bathing of the Shiva Lingam with sacred water and other offerings like milk, honey, ghee, and sandalwood paste.
- **Mangal Aarti**: Performed in the early morning, it is a unique ritual that fills the temple with the sound of bells, conch shells, and chants. The evening Ganga Aarti at the nearby Dashashwamedh Ghat is also a significant event for devotees.
- **Shraddha and Pind Daan**: Many pilgrims perform these rituals on the ghats of Varanasi for their ancestors, which are believed to bring peace to the departed souls.

The temple comes alive during various Hindu festivals, particularly:

Mahashivratri: Celebrated with grand enthusiasm, this festival honors the marriage of Lord Shiva and Goddess Parvati. Devotees fast, chant mantras, and perform night-long prayers.

Dev Deepawali: Known as the "Diwali of Gods," it is celebrated 15 days after Diwali, when the entire city is illuminated with lamps and diyas, creating a divine ambiance around the temple and ghats. The Kashi Vishwanath Temple offers a deep spiritual experience, inviting devotees to surrender their burdens to Lord Shiva and seek inner peace in the sacred city of Varanasi. Visiting the temple, combined with the city's ancient history and the divine Ganges, creates a powerful spiritual journey for any pilgrim.

2. Kedarnath Temple (Uttarakhand)

Kedarnath Temple, one of the holiest shrines dedicated to Lord Shiva, is located in the Garhwal Himalayas near the Mandakini River at an altitude of 3,583 meters (11,755 feet) above sea level. It is one of the twelve Jyotirlingas of Lord Shiva and holds immense spiritual significance in Hinduism. The temple is a crucial part of the Char Dham Yatra, a sacred pilgrimage in the Indian Himalayas, along with Badrinath, Gangotri, and Yamunotri. The temple is surrounded by the majestic Kedarnath range, offering breathtaking views of snow-covered peaks, which add to the aura of the temple. Due to its remote and high-altitude location, the journey to Kedarnath is considered a challenging but spiritually rewarding pilgrimage.

Mythological Significance

Kedarnath Temple is steeped in ancient Hindu mythology. It is believed to be the site where the Pandavas, the heroes of the Mahabharata, sought Lord Shiva's blessings to absolve themselves of the sins of killing their relatives in the Kurukshetra war. However, Shiva initially avoided them and took the form of a bull (Nandi) to remain hidden. When the Pandavas found him, he disappeared into the earth, leaving behind his hump, which is worshipped in the temple. Other parts of Shiva's body are worshipped at other locations in Uttarakhand, forming the Panch Kedar pilgrimage (Kedarnath, Tungnath, Rudranath, Madhyamaheshwar, and Kalpeshwar).

The temple's mythological connection with the Pandavas and its designation as a Jyotirlinga make it one of the most significant pilgrimage sites for devotees of Lord Shiva.

Architectural Features

The Kedarnath Temple is built using large, evenly cut grey stones, believed to date back to the 8th century, and was constructed by Adi Shankaracharya, the renowned Indian philosopher and theologian, to revive Hinduism in India. The original structure, according to legend, was built by the Pandavas.

Key architectural elements include:
- **Main Shrine**: The central deity of the temple is a triangular-shaped lingam, which represents the hump of Lord Shiva as a bull.
- **Mandapa (Assembly Hall)**: The mandapa is where pilgrims gather for prayers. The temple's interiors feature ancient carvings and images of deities and scenes from Hindu mythology.
- **Outer Structure**: The temple's stone walls and roof are known for their simple, sturdy construction, reflecting the ancient North Indian temple architecture.

The surrounding landscape of towering snow-clad mountains creates a mystical and spiritual environment that deeply touches devotees.

Spiritual Practices and Rituals
- **Abhishekam**: Rituals include the daily Abhishekam (bathing of the Shiva Lingam with sacred water and offerings), which is considered a deeply purifying act for devotees.

- **Aarti**: Special aartis are performed every morning and evening, when priests offer lamps, chants, and mantras in devotion to Lord Shiva.
- **Meditation and Reflection**: Due to the serene, high-altitude location, many pilgrims choose to meditate at the temple, seeking spiritual solace and inner peace.

Festival and Celebrations

- **Mahashivratri**: Like many other Shiva temples, Mahashivratri is celebrated with grandeur at Kedarnath, where devotees fast, chant prayers, and perform rituals to honor Lord Shiva.
- **Kedarnath Opening Ceremony**: The temple opens to devotees every year in April-May (Akshaya Tritiya) and closes in November (Kartik Purnima) for the winter season, when heavy snowfall makes the area inaccessible.

During the closure, the deity is transferred to Omkareshwar Temple in Ukhimath, where it is worshipped during the winter months.

In 2013, Kedarnath and the surrounding areas suffered devastating flash floods caused by a cloudburst and glacial overflow, which led to significant loss of life and infrastructure damage. Miraculously, the temple itself remained mostly intact, which many devotees saw as divine intervention. Since then, significant efforts have been made to rebuild and improve the region's infrastructure, ensuring better access and safety for future pilgrims.

Kedarnath Temple offers a unique blend of spirituality, adventure, and natural beauty, making it one of the most revered destinations for devotees of Lord Shiva. The journey to Kedarnath is not just a pilgrimage but also a testament to the devotion, endurance, and faith of those who make the trek to this remote and sacred shrine.

3. *Amarnath Cave Temple (Jammu & Kashmir)*

The Amarnath Cave Temple, located in the Indian union territory of Jammu & Kashmir, is one of the holiest and most ancient pilgrimage sites dedicated to Lord Shiva. It is renowned for the naturally occurring Shiva Lingam, made of ice, which forms inside the cave during the summer months. The lingam is considered a sacred symbol of Lord Shiva, and its annual formation is seen as a divine phenomenon by devotees.

Situated at an altitude of approximately 3,888 meters (12,756 feet) in the Himalayas, the Amarnath cave draws thousands of pilgrims every year during the Amarnath Yatra, a rigorous yet spiritually rewarding pilgrimage. The cave is surrounded by snow-clad mountains and offers a profound connection with nature and the divine.

Mythological Significance

The Amarnath Cave holds immense importance in Hindu mythology. According to legend, it is the place where Lord Shiva revealed the secret of immortality (Amar Katha) to his consort, Goddess Parvati. To ensure that no living being could hear this divine secret, Shiva left behind all his earthly possessions, including his bull (Nandi), his serpent, and his moon, and even placed his son Ganesha outside the cave. However, it is believed that two pigeons overheard the conversation and were blessed with immortality. Many pilgrims report seeing a pair of pigeons near the cave as a sign of divine presence.

This story makes Amarnath a symbol of the eternal nature of life, and pilgrims undertake the Yatra seeking Lord Shiva's blessings for liberation and spiritual awakening.

Spiritual Significance

The naturally formed ice Shiva Lingam, which changes in size depending on the moon's phases, is the central object of worship in the Amarnath cave. It is considered a physical manifestation of Lord Shiva. Two other ice formations next to the main lingam are believed to represent Goddess Parvati and Lord Ganesha, adding to the temple's sacredness.

The pilgrimage to Amarnath is viewed as a journey toward attaining moksha (spiritual liberation). The challenging trek and high-altitude conditions add to the spiritual intensity of the experience, with many pilgrims considering it a test of their faith, dedication, and endurance.

The Amarnath Yatra, held annually between June and August (Shravan month of the Hindu calendar), is the pilgrimage to visit the Amarnath cave. The Yatra is one of the toughest in India due to its high-altitude location, rocky terrain, and unpredictable weather.especially for those with health concerns.

Rituals and Ceremonies

The most important ritual at Amarnath Cave is the darshan (viewing) of the ice Shiva Lingam. Pilgrims offer flowers, fruits, and other offerings to the lingam and pray for blessings and spiritual growth.

- **Bam Bam Bhole**: The echoing chants of "Bam Bam Bhole" (a mantra invoking Lord Shiva) resonate throughout the journey, as pilgrims chant the sacred phrase during their trek to the cave.
- **Shravan Mela**: The Yatra coincides with the Shravan Mela, a major festival during the Hindu month of Shravan, when the Lingam is said to be at its largest.

Amarnath Cave and Natural Features
The cave is located in a stunning valley surrounded by glaciers and snow-covered peaks. The cold environment inside the cave allows for the natural formation of the ice lingam, which is typically at its peak during June and July. As the summer progresses and temperatures rise, the lingam gradually shrinks and melts away.

- **Sheshnag Lake**: Pilgrims on the Pahalgam route pass by Sheshnag Lake, a beautiful, high-altitude glacial lake. It is said to be the abode of the mythical snake Sheshnag, associated with Lord Vishnu and other Hindu deities.

- **Panchtarni**: Located near the cave, Panchtarni is a serene meadow surrounded by mountains, where pilgrims camp before undertaking the final leg of the journey to the cave.

The weather in the Amarnath region is highly unpredictable. The Yatra season often experiences rain and snow, and temperatures can range from warm during the day to freezing cold at night. Pilgrims are advised to be prepared for sudden weather changes and carry waterproof clothing, sturdy trekking shoes, and warm gear.

Spiritual Journey and Rewards
The Amarnath Yatra is seen as one of the most demanding yet spiritually fulfilling pilgrimages in India.
It is not just the darshan of the ice lingam that draws devotees but also the entire journey through the rugged and beautiful landscape, which symbolizes the spiritual ascent toward God. The Yatra serves as a test of both physical endurance and faith, allowing pilgrims to connect deeply with Lord Shiva and nature.
Visiting the Amarnath Cave Temple is an unforgettable experience that combines spiritual

devotion with the awe-inspiring beauty of the Himalayas, making it a pilgrimage that resonates with devotees on a profound level.

4. Somnath Temple (Gujarat)

The Somnath Temple, located in the coastal town of Prabhas Patan in Gujarat, is one of the most ancient and revered temples dedicated to Lord Shiva. It is considered the first among the twelve Jyotirlingas, making it one of the holiest shrines in Hinduism. The temple is known for its grand architecture, historical significance, and spiritual prominence. Somnath means "Protector of the Moon God" (Soma), reflecting the temple's deep-rooted mythological and religious connections. The temple has been destroyed and rebuilt several times throughout history, standing as a symbol of resilience and faith.

The temple's current structure was reconstructed in 1951 under the leadership of Sardar Vallabhbhai Patel, following its desecration during invasions.

Mythological Significance

The legend of Somnath is intertwined with the story of the Moon God (Chandra). According to Hindu mythology, Chandra was cursed by his father-in-law, Daksha Prajapati, to wane in brightness due to his preferential love toward one of his 27 wives, Rohini, over the others. To rid himself of the curse, Chandra prayed to Lord Shiva at the spot where the Somnath Temple stands today. Shiva, pleased with his devotion, partially relieved him of the curse, causing the moon to wax and wane. As a result, the name "Somnath" translates to "Lord of the Moon."

The story symbolizes the cyclic nature of time, with phases of waxing and waning representing the rhythm of life.

Historical Importance

The Somnath Temple has a storied history, with evidence suggesting that it existed as far back as 2000 BCE. It has been destroyed and rebuilt several times over the centuries, with major destructions caused by Mahmud of Ghazni in 1026 CE and subsequent invaders. Despite these attacks, the temple was always restored by devout Hindu kings, including Maharaja Bhimdev and King Kumarpal of the Solanki dynasty.

The current temple, rebuilt in the Chalukya style of architecture, was inaugurated in 1951 by India's first president, Dr. Rajendra Prasad. The temple's rich history is a testament to the unyielding faith of the people who continually revived it after periods of devastation.

Architectural Features

The modern Somnath Temple is a magnificent structure, built in the Chalukya style, characterized by intricate carvings, large courtyards, and towering spires. It showcases the skill and craftsmanship of ancient Indian temple architecture. Key features of the temple include:

- **Main Shrine**: The sanctum sanctorum houses the revered Shiva Lingam, which is worshipped as the Jyotirlinga of Somnath. Devotees from across the world come to seek Lord Shiva's blessings here.
- **Shikhara (Tower)**: The temple's massive tower rises to a height of about 50 meters (164 feet), and the temple's spire points directly toward the South Pole, symbolizing its spiritual alignment with the universe.
- **Carvings and Sculptures**: The temple walls are adorned with intricate carvings of Hindu deities, motifs, and historical scenes. The stonework reflects the grandeur of traditional Indian temple architecture.

- **Sagar Darshan**: The temple is located on the coast of the Arabian Sea, offering breathtaking views of the ocean. The sight of the temple against the backdrop of the sea creates an awe-inspiring spiritual atmosphere.
- **Jyotirlinga and Nandi**: Inside the garbhagriha (inner sanctum), the black stone lingam represents the eternal flame of Lord Shiva, and the temple also houses a large Nandi statue, Shiva's bull mount, which faces the sanctum.

Spiritual Practices and Rituals

- **Aarti and Abhishekam**: Daily aarti (ritual worship) is performed at the Somnath Temple, with specific ceremonies occurring during dawn, midday, and evening. **Abhishekam** (the ritual bathing of the Shiva Lingam) is a central part of the worship, where sacred water, milk, honey, and other offerings are poured over the lingam.
- **Shrawan Month**: The month of Shrawan (July-August) is considered highly auspicious for worshipping Lord Shiva, and the temple sees a surge in pilgrim numbers

during this time. Special prayers and events are held throughout the month.

Festivals

- **Mahashivratri**: The most significant festival celebrated at Somnath is Mahashivratri, which marks the night when Lord Shiva is believed to have performed the Tandava, the cosmic dance of creation, preservation, and destruction. The temple sees thousands of devotees participating in all-night vigils, chanting prayers, and offering rituals.

- **Somnath Fair**: Held during the Kartik Purnima (the full moon in the Hindu month of Kartik, usually November), the Somnath Fair is a vibrant festival, where devotees gather to celebrate with religious rituals, cultural performances, and processions.

The Somnath Temple not only stands as a symbol of religious devotion but also represents India's historical resilience. Its multiple reconstructions after destruction by invaders speak to the undying spirit of faith that surrounds this sacred place. Devotees believe that visiting Somnath brings them closer to Lord Shiva and helps them attain salvation.

For pilgrims, Somnath offers a serene yet powerful spiritual experience, where the divine presence of Lord Shiva is felt amidst the grandeur of history and the peaceful beauty of the Arabian Sea.

5. Mahakaleshwar Temple (Ujjain, Madhya Pradesh)

The Mahakaleshwar Temple, located in the ancient city of Ujjain in Madhya Pradesh, is one of the most significant and revered temples dedicated to Lord Shiva. It is one of the twelve Jyotirlingas, which are believed to be self-manifested representations of Shiva's infinite energy. The temple is especially unique because it is the only Dakshinamukhi Jyotirlinga (a Shiva Lingam facing south), symbolizing the lord's control over time, death, and the cosmic order.

Ujjain itself is one of India's most sacred cities, known for its ancient heritage, rich cultural history, and its connection with time (Kaal) as per Hindu cosmology.

The temple stands on the banks of the Shipra River, which holds religious significance, especially during the Kumbh Mela, a grand religious fair held every 12 years.

Mythological Significance

According to Hindu mythology, the temple is named Mahakaleshwar because Lord Shiva is considered the Lord of Time (Mahakal). The legend behind the temple's significance is closely tied to the myth of a demon named Dushana, who terrorized the people of Ujjain and disrupted their religious practices. The people prayed to Lord Shiva for protection, and in response, Shiva appeared in his fierce form as Mahakala and destroyed the demon. He then took residence in Ujjain as the city's eternal protector and ruler of time and death.

Mahakaleshwar represents the aspect of Lord Shiva that governs the cycles of time—creation, preservation, and destruction. Worship at this temple is believed to grant liberation from the cycle of life and death (moksha) and freedom from the fear of death.

Architectural Features

The Mahakaleshwar Temple showcases a blend of Rajput and Maratha architecture, with towering spires, detailed carvings, and a majestic facade. The temple's serene and ancient atmosphere is enhanced by its sacred surroundings and religious importance. Key architectural and spiritual features include:

- **Main Shrine (Garbhagriha)**: The sanctum sanctorum houses the Shiva Lingam, which is the focal point of devotion. It is uniquely positioned to face the south (Dakshinamukhi), a rare orientation symbolizing Shiva's control over death and time. The lingam is believed to be swayambhu (self-manifested), emerging naturally from the ground, unlike other man-made idols or lingams.
- **Temple Complex**: The multi-level temple complex is divided into three levels. The uppermost level is where the Mahakaleshwar Lingam is installed, while two other important shrines dedicated to Omkareshwar (another form of Shiva) and Nagchandreshwar are located in the temple's middle and top floors. The Nagchandreshwar temple opens only on Nag Panchami (a day to honor the serpent deity).
- **Spacious Courtyards and Pillared Halls**: The temple has expansive courtyards and

corridors that accommodate thousands of devotees during festivals. The walls and pillars are adorned with carvings of Hindu deities, motifs, and scenes from sacred texts.

Spiritual Practices and Rituals

Mahakaleshwar Temple is renowned for its elaborate rituals, especially the Bhasma Aarti, which is considered one of the most significant and unique worship practices in Hinduism.

- **Bhasma Aarti**: Performed in the early hours of the morning, this is the most distinctive ritual of the Mahakaleshwar Temple. **Bhasma** (sacred ash), traditionally made from burnt cow dung, is offered to the Shiva Lingam during this ritual. The ash is symbolic of the transient nature of life and the finality of death, underscoring Lord Shiva's power over time and mortality. The ritual begins at 4 AM and draws thousands of devotees who seek a special darshan of Lord Shiva during this time. Men are required to wear traditional dhoti to witness the aarti, and women are not allowed to enter the sanctum during this specific ceremony.

- **Shayan Aarti**: Performed in the evening, this is another important aarti (prayer ritual) where Lord Shiva is symbolically put to rest for the night. It is a serene and spiritually charged ceremony.
- **Rudrabhishek**: A powerful form of worship where devotees offer water, milk, honey, and other sacred items to the Shiva Lingam while chanting the Rudra Mantras. This ritual is believed to bring peace, prosperity, and divine blessings to those who perform it.
- **Maha Shivaratri**: The grandest festival celebrated at Mahakaleshwar Temple is Maha Shivaratri, marking the night when Lord Shiva is said to have performed the Tandava, the cosmic dance of creation and destruction. Thousands of devotees flock to the temple during this time, fasting and praying through the night in honor of Lord Shiva. Special pujas and processions are carried out throughout the day and night.

Religious Festivals

- **Shravan Maas (July-August)**: The month of Shravan is highly auspicious for Shiva worship, and the temple witnesses a surge in pilgrims during this period. Devotees offer prayers, conduct abhishekam, and seek Shiva's blessings for health, prosperity, and spiritual growth.

- **Nag Panchami**: On this day, the Nagchandreshwar temple located on the top floor of the Mahakaleshwar complex is opened for devotees, and special prayers are offered to Lord Shiva and his serpent companions.

Significance of Ujjain

The Mahakaleshwar Temple's location in Ujjain adds to its spiritual significance. Ujjain is one of the seven Moksha-puris (sacred cities that grant liberation) in Hindu tradition.

It is also associated with the Kumbh Mela, the largest religious gathering in the world, held every twelve years. The confluence of the sacred Shipra River with this ancient city adds to its religious importance, and pilgrims believe that a visit to Ujjain can help cleanse them of sins and lead them toward spiritual liberation.

A visit to the Mahakaleshwar Temple is not just a pilgrimage but a journey toward understanding the mysteries of time and existence. Worshipping

Lord Shiva in his Mahakal form is believed to bring peace, liberation from fear, and protection from the cycle of birth and death. The temple's powerful spiritual energy, coupled with its ancient heritage, makes it one of the most sought-after destinations for devotees seeking divine intervention and blessings for a prosperous life.

For those who seek moksha or salvation, a visit to Mahakaleshwar Temple in Ujjain is said to help them transcend the cycle of time and attain spiritual liberation.

These are just some of the most important Shiva temples in India, each carrying immense spiritual significance and cultural heritage. However, there are many more Shiva temples across the country, Each temple offers a unique connection to Lord Shiva and is revered for its own legends, rituals, and significance. The diversity of Shiva worship across India reflects the deep devotion to Mahadev, the eternal Lord of Time, Creation, and Destruction.

Chapter 15

Daily Worship Practices of Lord Shiva: Connecting with the Divine

Worshiping Lord Shiva is an ancient tradition rooted in devotion, mindfulness, and spiritual connection. Each aspect of the daily worship practices for Shiva holds deep symbolic meaning and is designed to elevate the devotee's consciousness while fostering a personal relationship with the divine. Here's a guide on how devotees can incorporate these rituals into their daily lives.

1. Chanting "Om Namah Shivaya"

The mantra "Om Namah Shivaya" is central to Shiva worship. It translates to "I bow to Shiva," where Shiva represents the inner self—the pure, transcendent consciousness.

How to Chant:

- Sit in a quiet place, preferably in front of a Shiva Lingam or a sacred space.
- Close your eyes and take a few deep breaths to center yourself.

- Begin chanting "Om Namah Shivaya" either silently or aloud.
- Chant for 108 repetitions using a mala (prayer beads) to maintain focus.

Spiritual Benefits:

- The vibration of "Om" harmonizes the body's chakras (energy centers), particularly the heart (Anahata) and throat (Vishuddha) chakras, leading to a balanced flow of spiritual energy.
- Regular chanting helps purify the mind, instills peace, and fosters a deep sense of devotion and inner stillness.

2. Offering Bilva Leaves

The Bilva (Bael) leaf is sacred to Lord Shiva and plays a vital role in his worship. Offering these trifoliate leaves symbolizes the surrender of body, mind, and soul to Shiva.

How to Offer:

- Wash the Bilva leaves with clean water.
- While chanting "Om Namah Shivaya," place the leaves one by one on the Shiva Lingam or in front of a Shiva image.
- Ensure that the leaves are offered with love, intention, and a pure heart.

Spiritual Significance:
- The Bilva leaf is said to cool Shiva's fiery aspect and is a symbol of spiritual purity.
- Offering these leaves is believed to cleanse past karmas and bring prosperity and well-being to the devotee.

3. Fasting for Shiva

Fasting, particularly on Mondays (Somvar) and during special occasions like Maha Shivaratri, is a common practice among Shiva devotees.

How to Fast:
- Devotees may choose to fast from sunrise to sunset, consuming only water, fruits, or specific light foods (known as *Phalahar*).
- During the fast, it's important to remain spiritually focused by reading Shiva scriptures, chanting, and avoiding distractions.

Spiritual Benefits:
- Fasting cleanses both the body and mind, heightening spiritual awareness and devotion.
- It serves as an act of penance and dedication, helping devotees surrender their worldly attachments in devotion to Shiva.

4. Meditation on Shiva

Meditation is an integral part of Shiva worship. It is believed that Lord Shiva, as the eternal yogi, embodies perfect stillness, making him a symbol of meditation.

How to Meditate:

- Sit in a comfortable position with a straight spine, either in a sacred space or a calm corner.
- Focus on an image of Shiva, the Shiva Lingam, or simply visualize him in your mind.
- Breathe slowly and deeply, focusing on the mantra "Om Namah Shivaya" or on Shiva's third eye, which represents spiritual wisdom.

Spiritual Benefits:

- Meditation on Shiva deepens inner peace, aligns the devotee with divine consciousness, and removes negative thoughts.
- It aids in self-realization and liberation, connecting the individual soul (Atman) with the universal consciousness (Paramatman).

5. Daily Rituals and Arti

Performing aarti (ritual of offering light) in front of Shiva is a powerful way to end daily worship.

How to Perform:
- Light a diya (lamp) with ghee or oil.
- After completing your prayers, wave the diya in a circular motion in front of the deity, symbolizing the light of knowledge and devotion dispelling darkness.
- Accompany the aarti with devotional songs or chants dedicated to Lord Shiva.

Spiritual Benefits:
- Arti signifies the removal of ignorance and the blessing of divine wisdom.
- It strengthens the devotee's connection to the divine, symbolizing the offering of oneself in service and humility.

The Essence of These Practices

Daily worship practices like chanting, offering Bilva leaves, fasting, and meditation are all paths to maintaining a deep personal connection with Shiva. These rituals help foster mindfulness and devotion, allowing devotees to transcend their mundane concerns and connect with the divine energy that Lord Shiva embodies. They serve as a reminder of Shiva's presence in all aspects of life—within the self, in nature, and in the cosmos.

By making these simple practices a part of their daily routine, devotees can experience a profound transformation, both spiritually and personally, as they align themselves with the peace, power, and wisdom of Lord Shiva.

Chapter 16

Shiva in the Modern World

In today's fast-paced, chaotic world, Lord Shiva's teachings and stories continue to hold profound relevance. His embodiment of detachment, wisdom, and the destruction of ego offers a spiritual guide for those seeking inner peace amid the constant rush of modern life. Shiva's ability to remain calm amidst chaos can inspire us to cultivate inner stillness and focus on what truly matters, shedding distractions and unnecessary attachments.

Shiva's detachment, as seen in his ascetic lifestyle, teaches us to let go of material desires and ego-driven ambitions. In a world obsessed with success, wealth, and status, his example reminds us that true fulfillment comes from within, from knowing the self and living authentically. His wisdom speaks to the importance of self-awareness, urging us to look beyond surface realities and cultivate a deeper understanding of life's essence.

Whether through meditation or mindfulness, the practice of slowing down and reflecting is invaluable in today's hyper-connected society. Moreover, Shiva's role as the destroyer of ego is especially significant. The ego, with its constant demands for validation, control, and superiority, can become a source of suffering. Shiva's fierce yet transformative destruction symbolizes the importance of dissolving this ego-centric mindset to open the door to higher consciousness. By embracing this aspect of Shiva, we can find liberation from self-imposed limitations and discover a more expansive, peaceful way of being.

Conclusion

Personal Reflections

On a personal level, Shiva's teachings have always resonated deeply with me. His presence, whether through meditation or reflection, has been a guiding force in my own life. The idea of releasing attachment to external outcomes, embracing change, and seeking wisdom within has brought me clarity and peace during challenging times. I have found that the lessons of Shiva, whether through his myths or his spiritual principles, are transformative for anyone on a spiritual journey. They encourage us to face life's storms with courage, dissolve the ego's grip, and ultimately discover the divine essence that lies within each of us.

Shiva, the eternal yogi, is not just a figure of the past but a timeless guide for navigating the complexities of the present. His wisdom offers a path to inner peace, helping us to reconnect with ourselves and the greater mysteries of existence.

www.ingramcontent.com/pod-product-compliance
Lightning Source LLC
Chambersburg PA
CBHW071012220526
45526CB00012B/82